The Mad Adventures of a First-time Dad
_____

The Mad Adventures of a First-time Dad

Written by Yashivan Govender

Edited by Robert Quarshie

Produced by Simon Nye

Copyright © 2015 by Yashivan Govender

Cover illustration by Sakhile Gumbi

All rights reserved. This book or any portion thereof may not be reproduced or used in any manner whatsoever without the express written permission of the publisher except for the use of brief quotations in a book review or scholarly journal.

First Printing: 2015

ISBN 978 0 620 65052 6

A FirstStep.me project
www.FirstStep.me

For more from The Fun Side of Being Serious visit www.Yashivan.com
The Fun Side of Being Serious: A FirstStep Guide to Online Business
The Fun Side of Being Serious: Go Global or Go Home

Also from FirstStep.me – The Breaking Stereotypes Documentary series
www.BreakingStereotypes.org

Contents

Introduction 1

Part 1: The nine month training camp to parenthood 3

Chapter 1   The guineafowl 5

Chapter 2   Preparation, cultural lessons and Mr Miyagi 8

Chapter 3   Awkward panic events and mood swings that would make a samurai flinch 11

Chapter 4   Planning and an endless well of advice........................... 16

Chapter 5   Six months down, three months to go – time to grow up and get serious... 20

Chapter 6   The last steps.. 23

Chapter 7   Overdue, but not like a library book 26

Chapter 8   The bulletproof feeling... 29

Part 2: Year 1 31

Chapter 9   The first three months 33

Chapter 10 The battle of the diaper and one of the greatest business models of all time... 37

Chapter 11 A bicycle shop, an increase in laundry and an endless amount of snow 39

Chapter 12 Prams, a blender, hospitals and being knocked out without a punch 41

Chapter 13 Longest journey in the shortest time and minding your language.. 44

Part 3: Tales and adventures of other dads 49

Introduction

I am no expert in fatherhood and certainly not a super dad, but there is no doubt of my aspiration to get there. I guess that is probably the best way to describe becoming a first time dad – it requires somewhat superhuman abilities. It involves crazy challenges, adventures around every corner and of course lots of diaper changing encounters of varying types of smells and textures! But before I put you off with potty business you can rest assured that after numerous such encounters, coupled with tons of practice, patience and good humour, being a father becomes second nature. You end up with the ability to rock a diaper change blind-folded with one arm tied behind your back, among other skills.

The first nine months of my wife's pregnancy took me from being a totally unprepared chap to a responsible family man. Furthermore, my first year of being a dad was then a combination of learning that I was not the boss in the father-baby relationship and that babies in general know a lot more than you can imagine.

Between running a business, living in a country where English is not a first language and of course raising a baby, my experience of being a dad became a little more than just a learning adventure.

Welcome to my mad adventures of a first time dad!

Disclaimer: This is just a guide and interpretation of my adventures as a parent. Seeking the correct medical advice and proper information is always best in terms of parenting. Most importantly every child is different. They all have individual needs and personalities.

Part 1: The nine month training camp to parenthood

Chapter 1
The guineafowl

A guineafowl, two South Africans, a Kiwi and a Bavarian all walk into a bar...and the joke somewhat ends with me becoming a father.

My foray into parenthood starts quite simply in the African bush: driving in a Jeep with a Kiwi of Sri Lankan heritage, a Jewish South African, a Bavarian and of course myself, the South African of Indian decent.

An interesting mix of cultures, enjoying interesting times in what was somehow a very tame safari. Sadly the only wildlife action we encountered (several times) on that day were numerous flocks of very odd, wild guineafowl.

Now as far as I am concerned, the guineafowl should be classified as a modern dodo. No offence to guineafowl lovers, but these birds are a confused and rather daft breed and top contenders for the Darwin Award. I say this because they are known for ingeniously protecting themselves from nocturnal predators by perching themselves on the lowest possible branch available on a tree. These modern day dodos, which happen to be an effortlessly captured delicacy among people in West Africa, also fail to understand the concept of ducking (no pun intended) for cover. Rather they prefer running in a straight trajectory from anything pursuing heavily at heels. This included the rather loud and gripping wheels of our travelling safari vehicle.

What I am getting at is that the short-lived life of a guineafowl can be attributed to a lack of foresight and planning – something every human is supposedly given by birth right, or so I thought.

As my team of mishmash adventurers travelled past numerous modern dodos and cracked as many jokes we could about the poor creatures, they ran seemingly headless around us as if we were long lost relatives returning to the flock. And then suddenly the sullen sound of a puncture gave an abrupt end to our poultry hysterics. So, with one knee on the dirt and my city boy attributes showing ever so present, I began to change the flat tyre of our Jeep.

It didn't take long for the Kiwi to unleash some verbal abuse, nor for one guineafowl to poke its nosey head into our driving misfortune and silently oversee the repair. As my contempt for the guineafowl grew stronger, my efforts at the tyre changing exercise plummeted, triggering the Kiwi to tag himself in as chief tyre changer. In no time he had us safely back on track on our adventure through guineafowl land.

From thereon, tyre-changing jokes went ahead of guineafowl mockery with me taking pole-position ahead of the modern dodo! So now outplayed by a guineafowl and mocked by a Kiwi, I figured life was showing me a sign, telling me to catch a wake up. Though I was totally oblivious to this at first, I realised soon after that that life was about to throw me a big, fat, swinging curve ball!

There are tons of literature, movies and advice about becoming a dad, father, papa or whatever you are being, or will be called by your little one. But not all such anecdotes have relevant advice. When I found out I was going to be a father, the (digital) pregnancy test indicated undoubtedly that my life was going to have a very lively addition to it. But was I ready to become a father? I didn't know then how to answer that.

I was still wrestling with the thoughts that only weeks earlier I couldn't change the tyre of an off-road vehicle and that a daft, smelly bird took me for its intellectual match. But if I couldn't change a tyre or mentally challenge the antics of a guineafowl, how was I possibly going to be able to raise a child and maintain a family? Minutes before that digital pregnancy test confirmed my suspicions - and yes every guy in a steady relationship is always suspicious of pregnancy, I was part of a group of young people enjoying the vanities of a risk-free social life. But it then slowly dawned on me that I would be joining the super cool dad's club! Okay so maybe I exaggerated the super cool bit but still this was a totally new and thrilling role to have in life.

Lessons learned

- Never volunteer to change a tyre unless forced to. If the option is available, let the Kiwi do it first up.
- Guineafowls are cheeky creatures.
- Digital pregnancy tests are interactive and rapid catalysts of ageing.

The guide: Manning up after finding out

Finding out that you are going to be a father is always unique and different for each man. No matter how unprepared you feel or think that you are in terms of becoming a father, the forces of nature via instincts and intuition will inevitably prepare you for the life changing evolution to fatherhood.

Sure you may not be the best father or parent around but there are no benchmarks or standards to rank your parental skills. The first and most critical part is not to make a run for it - leaving your partner to be a single parent. Even if you are not in a formal relationship, it is important to be as supportive as you can within the boundaries of your relationship or association with the other person. From basic pregnancy tests to the awkward gynaecological examinations, things will get a lot more adult-like in the next nine months of the pregnancy.

The first and most important step into fatherhood is to accept that you are going to be a father ("Hi, my name is Yashivan, and I'm going to be a dad.") What type of father you will be, is entirely up to you!

Chapter 2
Preparation, cultural lessons and Mr Miyagi

Finding out I was going to become a father kind of side-swiped me because at the time I was just only getting ready to become a loving husband. I had already asked my bride-to-be's parents if I could marry their daughter and with news of the baby, the pace hit warp speed. My soon to be in-laws lived in Germany and so a Skype call about the arrival of their first grandchild was met with various German celebratory phrases. Well I assume so because at that stage my comprehension of the German language was completely non-existent, so replying with a smile and nod seemed to be met with warm acceptance and I felt relieved. Closer to home, my parents' reaction to my phone call was not what I had in mind. My usual monthly call to my parents to tell them I was fine, healthy, working, eating and sheltering myself, seemed a long forgotten pastime of monotonous banter.

My father and mother each had their own unique response to their new grandchild and I wasn't expecting an overall bucket load of excitement from them. After all, I had been my own person since I left home at the age of 22. I knew as always that with my folks they needed time to digest things. This was a smacking difference between the two cultures of mine and my newly inducted German family.

In my case, the smacking difference or culture shock came about when I gave up my very settled, independent life and literally packed my bags for Germany. With a strong family support base in Bavaria, we hedged our bets on raising our growing family there. For me this was more than just a change in responsibilities but also a change in culture and lifestyle. My life before fatherhood involved a lot of travelling that resulted in a lot of time being spent in Europe. I had grown fond of Europe and it was no surprise that I married a European. I could see it now: the rolling hills and meadows, with chirping birds and that lady from *The Sound of Music* singing away in the not so far distance...

But I was so wrong: there I stood, in IKEA, lost and dumbfounded, no hills, no birds and no Julie Andrews. Just a lot of German-speaking people staring at me as though I was some kind of moving rare artefact. I always stared back at them often wondering what they were saying. Confusion is always best disguised with a warm smile, however what I got back was generally not the same gesture - cultural lesson (shock) 101!

By the time I left the non-stop action of IKEA and chugged back to my new home, I was definitely not keen on the idea that I would now have to assemble (by the boot load) an arson of baby gear. As most cars passed by me on the Autobahn as though I was Morgan Freeman with Jessica Tandy in tow (I grew up driving on the other side of the road!), my thoughts lingered on what to expect in the months ahead.

I arrived home and grappled with our new furniture which consisted of a wardrobe, baby cot both made of wood and a bunch of what my wife called 'essential' extras. By the time I had finished brutalising the wardrobe, my wife made a desperate attempt to save the cot from my impending abuse and stopped my next DIY attempt in its tracks. This of course sparked up a heated debate!

Which leads to family lesson 101: when proving ones manliness in the middle of an argument, one should not involve the dialogues like:

Wife: "Where did you learn to paint?!"

Me: "From Mr Miyagi when he taught Daniel Son how to paint the fence!"

Lessons learned

- Parents are an interesting breed of people: you grow up with them and then you become one of them.
- Telling your parents that you are going to be a parent can be like telling Batman he is dressed like a Bat, it could go either way!
- IKEA is like LEGOLAND for grown-ups!
- Driving as fast as you think you have ever driven is probably comparably really slow on the Autobahn.
- When in Europe, drive on the right-hand side of the road!

- Mr Miyagi was played by Noriyuki "Pat" Morita in the Karate Kid and his painting lessons are only good for self-defence! He remains my favourite teacher of all time.

The guide: Preparation – the man's guide to nesting

Bachelors go through various phases in their lives, the first phase is moving out of their parent's home into the first place of their own. This may be alone or with friends or flatmates and then eventually leads to phase two of living: either continue on your own (as you get sick of people eating your food or being ultra-messy), or move in with your significant other. These phases are combined with various and necessary improvements in one's life.

One such improvement would be 'downgrading' from the sporty vehicle that you thought was so awesome to that now spacious family car – and yes you can compromise by buying the sports versions like I did. The general rule is: if it can fit a baby seat in the back, argue all you want but you have a family car – no matter how much horsepower it has!

In the house you may want to stubbornly keep your gadgets and gizmos however you do so at your own risk as they will be eventually broken or treated like footballs soon enough by your child. You will be amazed at how far things that you treated with such care can "travel" through the machinations of a growing baby.

The next phase is making sure you have enough space for your new addition. Yes babies do take up space, which means getting extra housing space. Moving to a bigger location or making space within your current setup is probably the way to go. If you can get family support, it is worth it but that is really up to you (based on your level of tolerance and dependency on parents). Whatever the case may be, you need to create an environment that provides enough room for you and your family to grow in the early stages.

Chapter 3
Awkward panic events and mood swings that would make a samurai flinch

Giving up my independent life was interesting yet not easy. From the freedom and flexibility to dash out and do something, as well as having all the time in the world to plan a day, week or month ahead, all went out of the window. I found that time was a luxury that got depleted pretty quickly!

Welcome to panic at the disco, except this is not about a cool rock band...

Trying to act natural while sitting in the waiting room at a gynaecologists´ office is outright awkward. Everyone smiles at you with a warm grin except the few male visitors who tend to be less kindly and rather more fidgety. Making eye contact with them revealed looks of lost sheep rather than men confident that they had spawned the world´s next superhero. By the way: thinking your child is the next superhero of the universe is normal, but that's a story for later.

Of course there are the seasoned professionals out there when it comes to child rearing – so the fathers of two, three or even four kids tend to sit around the waiting room looking like they own the joint. One could imagine them rocking a baby carrier while pushing a pram and spinning a baby bottle on their finger-tips just to gloat. I couldn't help but acknowledge the very seasoned look of their significant others, who seemed to be (and most likely are) the ones in control of the tense situation.

Then you have rookies such as me, who pretended to read the pamphlets and counted the minutes as though counting down the arrival of the next millennium or doomsday. In my case, I was still playing in the minor leagues and my lack of experience seemed very obvious when I was reprimanded for playing around with medical equipment in the examination room by both the consulting doctor and my wife!

It ultimately dawned on me (again) that I was going to be a father on a more serious note when I saw the first ultrasound of my child. As beautiful as it looked and such a lovely feeling I felt, panic crept in while staring at the grainy ultrasound and thinking soon that the pea-like object I was looking at was soon going to evolve into a watermelon and then into a university student haggling for petrol money or worse yet…for beer!

I too was once a haggling university student to my parents and I didn't want another me on the horizon. I started making mental notes, thinking of various events that shaped and changed my life and how I would make sure I do them differently or better when I became a parent so that my pea, watermelon or haggling student didn't have to face similar challenges.

I also made very important notes of not doing what my parents did at times with me. One example is when my father tagged along on a date! I had just got my driver's licence and the old man refused for me to pick up a date unaccompanied because he felt I was too inexperienced a driver. It was the worst date of my life which oddly included us watching the aptly titled movie: "How to Lose a Guy in 10 Days" – in my case it took about ten minutes.

The panic subsided when I looked at the ultrasound picture again. The pea somewhat reassured me that its past, present and future will all be a different life to mine and I that I needed to ensure I was a dependable parent and not one that hid the car keys.

As time progressed, I was reminded that the baby would be arriving soon on numerous occasions as my wife's mood swings started to get more volatile. The encounters were swift, severe and took no prisoners. A samurai warrior would take down an opponent with the precision of a well-trained assassin - I however was spared no such luck. When the hormones erupted, I always somehow found myself in the middle of its path. I tried to duck and dive, avoid eye contact, even make a run for it to a safe hiding place.

I would often trigger a mood swing by mentioning a sore back or neck. Her personality would immediately change from being very pregnant and fragile to very pregnant and vengeful. Needless to say my back and neck pains quickly dissolved.

Once the Hormones shouted at me for buying the wrong type of milk. I didn't understand the actual type because it was written in German. An excuse which didn't even make it to the closing arguments!

Instead I learnt to resort to nodding in agreement and being silent, taking the blame for whatever the mood swing had in mind. I also came to terms with the fact that I wasn't dealing with my wife - I was dealing with something totally different so the key was to never take it personally. A lesson that l wish I had learned so much earlier!

There was an upside to the Hormones and mood swings though, and that was food cravings: I got to eat cool and yummy stuff with her so all was not lost!

Lessons learned

- Ultrasounds are cool; they tend to resemble watching a space movie.
- Playing with ultrasound equipment is not allowed or advised! Being shouted at by both doctor and wife in this regard is apparently a common rookie mistake.
- Some fathers like to show off that they are super awesome dads but one can generally spot the real responsible partner watching prudently over his shoulder.
- You can't help yourself but try and make mental notes of your parental encounters while growing up.
- Hormones are mean!
- Running away from a mood swing is a short term solution. Rather remain still or calm and try not to make eye contact.
- Try counting to ten, or if needed twenty, when facing Hormones. That little pause provides a buffer to deal with things rationally – and one of you needs to!
- Learning different types of baby powdered milk types in German can be tricky. There are tons of different brands, types and versions that is often available at the local grocery store.
- Food cravings are awesome!

The guide: Visit the gynaecologist...not just once. And good luck with mood swings!

Visiting the gynaecologist can be an awkward experience for a rookie. You almost feel like Darth Vader, with everyone looking and thinking: "Dude, why is he dressed like a robot and breathing so heavily?"

This is a place where you keep quiet, make minimal eye contact and try to absorb as much of the literature on offer. From pamphlets and magazines to books and even wall charts – the gynaecologist's waiting area is a repository of reproductive information. They drive home the point that you are not the only person there and that the most important person is your partner and the little one growing inside of her.

For healthy babies, emergency cases and even dealing with the loss of a baby, this is the hub of where things baby are monitored and your baby's development is mapped. One can only hope that your child will grow up to be healthy and strong. Be prepared for unexpected complications with the pregnancy, which are not easy processes to deal with, but be strong and seek the correct medical advice as a positive step forward in dealing with them.

The next important challenge to trust the knowledge and expertise of your consulting doctor. Your birth plan comes down to a personal choice based on what you and your partner feel most comfortable with. As Luke trusted Yoda in the famous George Lucas epics, the same sort of thinking applies. Well kind of. I doubt a green midget gynaecologist is going to convince anyone with a sound birth plan. While you are breaking new ground, this is probably all routine for your doctor. Make sure you ask lots of questions during your visits. In any case this is going to be a new routine for you, so strap on your seatbelts and be prepared to make regular trips to this place!

There is no real answer to dealing with Hormones. The best thing is to acknowledge is that like in a fight with Mike Tyson - you will come off second best. So don't mess with a mood swing because it can knock you out, wake you up and knock you out again. Trying adding in a buffer such as a rational count to ten or twenty before engaging in an argument which probably is not worth getting into in the first place! And empathise: your partner is probably more scared than you are as her body changes rapidly. A foot or shoulder rub can go a long way (don't even think of asking her to give you one!)

Remember the cool factor of the hormonal imbalances: food cravings. This means you get to snack and munch out your stress on some extra goodies too.

Chapter 4
Planning and an endless well of advice

I found that after the ultrasound and that splash-of-water-to-the-face moment, my game got a lot better and lot more serious. I guess it was my mind set that needed changing just like embarking on a business venture or in a major sporting event. But this wasn't a career changing milestone - this was a life changing one. I had to make sure I was ready to handle whatever was thrown at me – I didn't want to drop the ball. The scary part was that my wife had this mind-set from day one. I guess I was slow off the mark, but rather late than never!

I started reading pregnancy, baby and biology books. The one that I found really worthwhile was *Conception, Pregnancy and Birth* by Dr Miriam Stoppard. It explained everything from start to finish and kept it simple. As I mentioned earlier, there is a ton of literature out there so whatever works for the individual is best – coupled with sound professional advice of course! All I know is that what I learned in high school biology didn't often come close to what I was going through in the pregnancy. But then again, I never paid much attention at school so perhaps maybe it was just me.

While my wife was attending weekly birth classes held by the local midwife, I was still finding my way around my new surroundings. I was working from home - one of the most undervalued factors of the Internet and Wi-Fi age that allows for flexibility in the work environment. In my case this was even more conducive as my work was within the online business - I was running an online media company. On top of this, I was also going to German classes which at times were extremely entertaining. It was a class of total misfits either looking for a new life, had followed their significant other to Germany or in some cases just simply wanted to learn the language. In my case, I was the only one married to a German. However, we all had one common (or rather uncommon) factor – no one spoke the same language. The American and I spoke English, while the Italians and Greeks often verbally abused the Hungarian, who didn't understand so she just smiled back and laughed.

How we actually managed to learn anything was due to the patience and careful coordination of our teacher who spoke a bunch of languages and was a willing referee in much of the multi-lingual arguments. What seemed like a scene from the classic TV show *Mind Your Language* turned out to be a home away from home, giving me a much needed break away from the serious nature of work and my soon to be duties of fatherhood.

The other uncommon denominator that separated me from the odd bunch was that I was the only person who was going to be a father. Again I found myself wondering if there was there a message or memo that I had missed out on…

There are a lot of people who are veteran parents, which means they have a lot of advice and stories to tell; not just small stories but really big and epic ones. Some epic enough to scare you into wondering if children exist only to enact life-threatening feats. Others stories gave me the impression that some parents lived their lives entirely through their children – a cautionary tale.

Once I opened Pandora´s box by asking other parents for advice, it never closed and I learned to filter what was good and what was not. And if you are wondering there is such a club known as the cool parenting club. Admission is free and leads to an endless amounts of birthday parties, clowns, jumping castles. Before you start to panic, all this starts slowly and gains momentum later on. At this stage I was just glad that other people had been in this boat and that I wasn't venturing on some unchartered journey. The common factor - unlike my rather diverse and no common ground German language class - was that everyone would say being a parent was an awesome experience.

Sadly, some of the seasoned campaigners had some of their life ambitions fall by the way side, which was often characterised by an empty gaze at that stage of the conversation.

While I was researching my way forward and trying to get settled into Bavarian culture which included numerous attempts by various locals to get me to wear lederhosen, my wife was planning and preparing like a trooper. In her view, quality planning meant that our child would grow up in a stable environment while my focus was on affordability so our child would have a good economic future. We somehow met halfway. From eco-friendly baby monitors that emitted no radiation, to a car seat that looked like something well suited for the Bat Mobile. After a few loud 'discussions' we managed to reach a few settlements on which pram and a particular food processor to purchase. Somehow she always came out best in these discussions leaving me with a similar gaze to those parents who had given up on life ambitions.

We were altogether ready for our new arrival, we had gone through all the checklists from baby gear, accessories, even making sure that all stuff we had met the health and safety standards. We were after all in Germany where everything is stereotypically done to procedure, so I had faith in our all acquisitions! I even went out and bought a bunch of baby proofing contraptions, which happen to be in my case adult proof as well - they just don't tell you that on the box!

Lessons learned

- Reading up and asking advice on babies and being a parent tends to open a door to an endless amount of information. Sometimes you have to filter out the seeds from the melon.
- Learning a new language is sometimes a good distraction from becoming a parent. Get yourself a hobby.
- Arguments about mundane baby gear happen more often than you think!
- I don't think I will ever look good wearing lederhosen.
- Don't underestimate the value of a baby shower – you will get loads of baby gear you will need, and some stuff you never knew existed!

The guide: Following a detailed plan as Sherlock Holmes would solve a mystery

Research is always a good thing, and there are bucket loads of information out there. On the Internet, your questions are just a Google or Bing search away. When it comes to books, ones like

Conception, Pregnancy and Birth and *What to Expect when Expecting* are good reads. Other parents can offer good advice, and of course the expert advice of your consulting gynaecologist or midwife should always be at the top of your list.

There are so many things to take into consideration these days when it comes to getting baby gear. There are different safety, user and health standards that help to rank various gear suited for your new addition – again, research what you buy. Naturally, with the rise of the Internet, you are able to compare and purchase baby accessories a lot easier digitally, but going to a physical store and getting your hands on a pram or buggy is important because you will be using this equipment literally every day until your baby is ready to take 100 metre trials. Get a checklist, a budget and prioritise your needs, and if you are lucky you will be given the bulk of your gear from friends and family. By the time you are complete, including the baby proofing of your living quarters, you will feel as organised as the Batman of dads!

Chapter 5
Six months down, three months to go – time to grow up and get serious

As I battled further attempts to get me to wear lederhosen and fumbled with baby proof contraptions, I found myself slowly growing up. Slowly being the key word - if I was stunted at high school, university was just high school on steroids for me, but entering the working world was when life hit me with the biggest wake up call. I was running my own business from my final year of university and I was fully committed by the time I got my degree.

With a company based online I was able to journey to various parts of the planet while keeping the pulse behind my company very much alive. I literally put the idea of running a business from the moon to the test; however, I was waiting for a rocket ship to send me up. Real life was clawing its way inexorably into my adulthood with growing responsibilities. My previous life was just a passing flash, a blink of the eye, everything felt and seemed like lessons leading me towards fatherhood. Mr Miyagi's pearls of wisdom weren't so far away from my thoughts – it was really time to get serious!

I found myself cutting to the chase in business looking for better, more constructive results in the projects I ran. At the same time, I started to fall into a routine with fewer distractions: fatherhood was becoming more and more like business with my family being the focal project. As in business, you will make and lose friends, and sometimes unfortunately even family. I will never forget the phrase "You can count the people you trust most by the number of fingers on your hands." I noticed that my life changes were somehow mirroring my business changes. This was an interesting way to perceive life but it armoured me well for the journey ahead. I also found myself repeating "we are expecting" or "we are pregnant" - oddly enough it made sense in my head no matter how unnatural it sounded! It meant I had found the balance that I needed to make sure I could work effectively and manage my family's needs as well. Miyagi would be proud, after all a kitchen table is just as good as an office desk!

My wife's career was taking shape as well and between us there was a mutual understanding that we needed to coordinate our plans in such a way that we could cope with whatever lay ahead. From getting up earlier in the morning to meet deadlines to not sleeping at all to complete such deadlines - work seemed to have more meaning. It was the relentless pressure that the business had to work because you have everything on the line.

Of course I missed the mad days of running around causing havoc as any young lad would do, but those feelings soon passed. Instead, every night I would read to the belly of my wife the classics that I grew up with and hoped that I would become a recognised voice to my child's developing ears. It was my escape and my small way of sculpting a positive future for my baby. My wife would play music to the belly - all sorts, from classical to some out-the-box mixed CDs. One that seemed to surround the nine months of pregnancy was a Best of Reggae mix which she had grown accustomed to. Often I would go to sleep with the chilled beats of a reggae melody in my head.

Lessons learned

- Finding a balance between work, a career and family life as early as possible is really important.
- Reading to a baby can take you back to your favourite classic tales of literature!
- The Internet is the new flexible tool to become a stay at home dad to both work and help with family management.
- Growing up is not easy but somehow you find the time to reflect on life's lessons and have those light bulb moments.
- Referring to a pregnancy as "we are expecting" or "we are pregnant" is totally acceptable!

The guide: The Internet and balance

The Internet has allowed parents to work from home either partly or fully, thus creating the flexibility to cope with both family and their careers. But this also means that every hour counts.

Have fun and enjoy reading and interacting with your child while it is swimming and jumping around in your wife's belly. This is just the beginning of enjoying a second childhood, from music, books and gentle massaging of the belly; these are priceless moments of being a father and becoming a family.

Chapter 6
The last steps

Perhaps we prepared everything a little too early because the last three months seemed to take forever. The belly of my wife was nice and round - often we could see a kicking foot or a punching fist through the belly. Kicking and such manoeuvres had become a regular occurrence and though it was exciting at first it was a constant reminder that something awesome was on the way into my life.

We had decided that we wanted to know the sex of the baby early on ("It's a girl!"). As I watched my daughter in awe via ultrasound during our many check-ups, I couldn't help thinking about the inevitable teen years and some hormonal teenage boy rocking up at the door to date her! That scene from *Bad Boys 2* with Will Smith and Martin Lawrence wreaking havoc with a poor young lad trying to date Lawrence's character's daughter was the only reference I had to a situation like this!

I surfaced from the brief daydream realising that I would have years to prepare myself for that day of opening the door and being the overwhelming father that never would approved of anything that might be standing before him. So began my cold stare at the mirror exercise - practicing my Dwayne 'The Rock' Johnson eyebrow raise. I mean, who better to mimic than a muscle-bound, successfully intimidating WWE (World Wrestling Entertainment, Inc.) superstar?

Then came my movie preparation. The eighties and early nineties were home to oddball family and coming-of-age parenting movies. From Hugh Grant in *Nine Months* to Tom Selleck in *3 Men and a Baby*. Though I found these humorous, the situations these unfortunate men found themselves in were somewhat frightening. *Father of the Bride* with Steve Martin had two parts that fast tracked me into a spin.

It was Seth Rogen who brought a freshness to parenthood with the movie *Knocked Up*, which seemed brutally honest to me. For no matter how much reggae music I had in my life, things were never calm nor steady during the nine months of pregnancy – it wasn't a Hollywood masterpiece.

My wife luckily never suffered from morning sickness but rather suffered from dealing with various smells. Gorgonzola cheese is now a banned substance in our household forever. And as for the mood swings well, they came, left, returned, stayed, annoyed and then left and returned again. It was sort of like being a parent with a teenager, but we got through them. My wife didn't need the external preparation like I did since she had a physical reminder with her constantly. She represented the cool and consistent opposite to my uncertain self.

The settled feelings and calm waters my wife had brought forward took a huge turn for us when we went to visit the hospital where we had planned to have the baby delivered. A hospital is always an interesting place: you notice how people look at each other wondering what the other has and whether it is contagious or not. We on the other hand were noticing something else! It was a procedure that we had to have – the check-up with the consulting gynaecologist at the hospital – during this process we found that my daughter was in fact a dude! ("Oh wait, it's a boy!")

Upon hearing the 'boy wonder ' news, a smile as huge as the moon arrived on my face, mainly because I was tired of trying to master the Dwayne Johnson eyebrow impression. It didn't honestly matter what the sex of the baby was, but it was nevertheless a total surprise as we had gone all out gearing up for a girl over the past few months. With spectacular thoughts of doing awesome father and son activities running through my head, the look on my wife's face was one who thought her husband had gone loopy. I had explained to her that I didn't want to go through teenage adolescence drama with a daughter; she gently stroked my arm reassuringly and said something along the lines of - there is still time for more children. Talk about being unnecessarily pre-emptive!

After a while my near heart failure at the thought of any forthcoming children slowly dissolved. I started playing the name game with my wife with the hope of at least winning one debate over the nine months. My attempts at a resounding victory when it came to naming our boy were, however, firmly stonewalled. Suggestions such as Yashivan the 2nd, Thor (after the God of Thunder) and Junior (after a West Indian cricketer named Junior Murray) where all mercilessly put to the sword. We finally settled on picking a name that would represent his heritage from both Europe and Asia and at the same time would be fitting enough to be upheld by half a South African and half a German. Quietly though in my mind he was my little Superhero!

Lessons learned

- No matter how much I try I can't raise my eyebrow as well as Dwayne 'The Rock' Johnson!
- Ultrasounds have surprises for you including an umbilical cord hiding the 'reproductive organ' of a baby!
- Naming a baby after a former West Indian cricket player doesn't go down well with a German wife!
- Nor does the name Thor – God of Thunder!

The guide: Surprises and the name game

Finding the best birth place that fits your needs and the comfort of your baby is really up to the needs of the mother and the child. One hears about underwater births and some other methods that induce The Rock-like eyebrow rise. Being fussy about the where can be unnecessary as some people don't even get to the place when the baby arrives too quickly. Choose one that is swiftly reachable and cross your fingers you get to your desired delivery station in time.

Every day is different within the nine months and surprises are always around the corner, so try and be ready for whatever is thrown at you, good or bad. The key is to be flexible, to be supportive of your partner and to be as helpful as possible!

Naming your child is different for every parent but what does help is to have a name that can't be turned into a cruel nickname!

Chapter 7
Overdue, but not like a library book

Nine months had passed by and we were anxiously expecting our little one anytime; but anytime was not coming. More annoying was that for most of the month he was due, we would receive text messages, emails and phone calls asking if the little one had arrived. The answer was always no; out of frustration I would fabricate a story saying we just had twins. This would especially leave my wife's grandmother utterly confused mainly I think because she didn't understand my English or in this case what had now manifested into Denglish - a combination of German (*Deutsch*) and English. My mom didn't care for my jokes either, while my father often muttered something in the background about growing up.

Humour aside, my wife looked like she carried the world on her shoulders and being pregnant for yet another day would be all she could take! We had been told that if we didn't go into labour soon we would have to induce labour. This is something I was not ready for and though I had read it was a normal procedure, I still had reservations.

My reservations however meant nothing to my wife, who was ready to do whatever it took to get the baby out. And then on a day of a very long walk through the local town centre after a hearty breakfast and some much needed purchasing of flowers, her water broke! We had a comprehensive birth plan, well I think we did, but the moments went by in a flash and then were followed by what seemed like a slow motion journey to the hospital. We had prepared a full breakdown of who was going to drive us to the hospital - in this case it was my father in-law. Bags were packed for various emergencies and phone messages (pre-saved) of who needed to be notified for the arrival of the little one. The journey to the hospital felt like we were standing on the doorstep of something epic and amazing. My wife had kept calm and her calmness had almost sent me off to sleep - not surprisingly the reggae music was playing in the car.

My parents-in-law greeted us at the hospital, but only hung around for an hour before they decided to head home, leaving me in a literal state of shock. I thought they were staying for the whole show and would wait in the waiting area. As seasoned campaigners, they had better insight into what to expect. What we didn't expect, however, was nearly twenty hours of labour!

My wife is a very composed person. How she manages to stay that way is beyond me, as dealing with me as a husband with my madcap adventures in life and business would drive anyone dilly. Perhaps that is what makes us compatible: her tolerance mixed with my haphazardness. So when she remained totally calm throughout the labour process, it surprised everyone from the doctors to the midwives who didn't believe that she was so far along. Flash forward to the next morning and as we headed towards midday things began to take shape. I somehow managed to remain unruffled right up and until the point when my wife demanded the epidural.

As cool as a cucumber, the anaesthetist breezed into the delivery room and spoke to my wife as casually as though he was just there to remove a plaster from a scratched knee. But what he pulled out next was a needle that looked like it could take out a horse and not just sedate a pregnant woman! As I squirmed and looked into my wife's eyes, she remained motionless – not even signalling an ounce of pain. The truth is I was looking into her eyes because I was too afraid to watch the epidural procedure. She later told me that the contraction pains were so strong that they outweighed the epidural, so she never felt the needle. It didn't take much more time before it was 'all stations ready' and the little man was on his way.

Lessons learned

- Water breaking is not at all what it sounds like!
- Water breaking should be changed to a different phrase or term!
- Epidural needles are scary and women who have them put into them are super brave!

The guide: Welcome to labour

Most Hollywood movies make labour out to be a funny and eventful procedure. However, it isn't and at times you really have to take a step back to acknowledge that this whole process has nothing to do with you and it is all about making sure you are able to support your partner.

A birth plan is always good to have. Well, at least a strategy of what to expect or do during labour and the birth process. It is not inconceivable that a birth plan can completely fall by the wayside during all the action that is happening! Knowledge of medication and procedures like an epidural will make you feel less anxious, but the overall key is to make sure you are in safe medical hands.

Chapter 8
The bulletproof feeling

During the labour process, we were sent back and forth between our room and the delivery room. It was agonising because you knew anytime soon that you would literally be a father, a parent and a responsible human being – precisely when this would happen was open to fate and medicine! Sometime during our room shuffling, I received two phone calls, both from good friends with advice and ideas of what to expect. That is when I first heard the concept of a new born baby looking like an alien! Yes you heard correctly, an alien. These were the words I was being told moments before delivery time - not much of an inspiration and downright frightening! This was in contrast to the movies where you always find the baby looking like it was covered in angel dust and smelling like roses. What actually happens couldn't be further from the silver screen.

We arrived in the delivery room for the final time with all stations at full alert - midwives running around and a spectacled obstetrician pacing the floor as though he was expecting a delivery from DHL. However there was no parcel to be delivered but rather a full set of medical procedures that I still have no clue about. The midwives readied my wife for delivery and the game plan changed to her finishing off the final play! My wife was so brave and seemed to be the one giving me strength right up until I looked over to observe the delivery of my son! Only Ridley Scott could have prepared a better scene, although in my eyes he looked like he was covered in fairy dust and smelled like a bouquet of roses.

He had jet black hair, blue eyes and a set of lungs that could shatter amour-plated glass windows, just as you could imagine Thor would have done! To me the room sounded like the happiest place on the planet and everything was settling back into place and coming into life just like the Earth does after a storm. My wife was smiling and crying and I…well, I felt bulletproof! Nothing in the whole world could have altered my feelings nor stop my smiling for hours thereafter. My little Thor, my little superhero, my junior was here and he most certainly did not look alien!

After he was measured, weighed and examined, we went back to our recovery room. I ran back to the delivery room and hugged each of the people that helped us and kept thanking them. Though they had no clue what I was saying (in my excitement I spoke very rapid English; I didn't care), I was 29 years old and had finally found out that life and the whole world was preparing me to be able to handle everything that now lay ahead of me.

Hours went by, family and friends came through, we couldn't stop gazing at the baby; we didn't know what to expect next and everything he did was met with admiration. When he yawned, we smiled, when he opened his eyes, we let out a gasp; we were mushy and clichéd, but didn't care. Sometimes it's okay to spit out the gum guard and man down a little!

Lesson learned

- DHL is owned by the German postal service – true story.

The guide: From delivery and into your arms

There are loads of videos you can watch to help you prepare for the reality of labour and childbirth. The more you know before stepping into the delivery room, the better prepared you will be to deal with the process.

One often hears of people not making it in time to the hospitals or having emergency labour and deliveries – sometimes in the middle of nowhere. These stories make you breathe a sigh of relief when you are lucky enough to get it right.

Part 2: Year 1

Chapter 9
The first three months

From the moment that my son arrived he let us know he was around with his powerful set of lungs and his eyes that seemed both worldly and hungry to learn as much as he could. Our time at the hospital where he was born felt like going to university. It was a five-day crash course of what to do and what not to do with your baby. The doctors and nurses would sit in as Jedi Masters while we learned various un-Jedi-like tasks. What we didn't know was that our new baby had other plans. The first nine months was only boot camp for what was going to be a mad parenting adventure ahead.

"Junior", as I liked to call him (actually I had a bunch of nicknames for him, but this was my favourite), fell asleep during the journey home and stayed asleep for the next 6 hours. My wife (who was still recovering from the ordeal of labour) lay awake next to his cot while I passed out. The truth was that I hadn't slept properly in over a week and though I missed the uniqueness of a hospital bed having so many different positions, I hit slumber-land very fast.

I remember it so vividly probably because it was the last full-length sleep I had for the next year! Our bed stood next to the cot, but my rule of the baby sleeping in his own bed was not as much of a rule as it was a challenge to see how long the baby could last without having to be cuddled by his parents. With regular visits from the local midwife, it seemed as though we had things under control and the first month flew by in what was felt like seconds.

Summer had arrived with a vengeance of scorching heat and the evenings were brighter than I was used to. In South Africa, the sun sets between 6 pm and 8 pm, however the European summer days steal a few hours from the darkness of the night. My nights were categorised into various phases: wake up to the cry of the baby, play rock, paper, scissors with the wife and lose; crawl out of bed, find baby who was either in his cot or had somehow found his way into our bed, sing baby to sleep with a song, which as far as I am concerned would keep anyone awake as I am the best tone deaf singer in the world.

I was often chanting the universal "shhh, shhh, shhh" lullaby while cradling my boy as if he was made of delicate porcelain. This made my sister-in-law's boyfriend, who happened to be visiting us while he was on university vacation, complain that he was falling asleep when I was putting my son to sleep using the above mentioned method during the day. But while he took this as a nuisance to his university holiday experience, I took it as a compliment for one of the skills that I was developing as a Jedi Father!

During the summer, I discovered that most of the locals, including my sister-in-law's boyfriend, would go into vacation mode, and I would often find people lounging around with not much work to do. When there was sunshine available people scrambled to get as much of it as possible. As a brown man from the southern hemisphere, I found this odd and still do not quite understand it. In South Africa when it was hot, I would stay in the shade to keep cool - an action which never gained any acceptance here from the Bavarians.

As the summer continued beating the sweat out of me, the night's warmth also uncomfortably reminded me of my Indian heritage – indirectly telling me to man up. The nights raced by and I found more ingenious ways of winning the rock, paper scissors battles: mainly by pretending to be unconscious. We also managed soon enough to wake up every morning for the day as though we had slept through the night without any breaks in our sleep. It was an interesting feeling, and somehow I managed to get through work deadlines, assist with the baby and kept up with my German language classes. And while my German wasn't really improving further than the basics, the American in the class kept me entertained with his mad adventures of discovering various German beers. His anecdotes of beer adventures where both engaging and tempting. I would often leave class with the jealous thought that beer tasting would be the ultimate way of integrating into Bavarian culture. But this was a contrasting picture of my life, which involved watching my son fighting for boobs in his quest to have breast milk at his beck and call.

By the third month, I realised that summer was going to end and though the months of summer had over-stayed its welcome, I already began to wish it would continue. Junior found his rhythm and we developed a routine that we believed would never stay in place long enough to become a habit.

During the day while I worked at my desk (the kitchen table), I had him wrapped onto me or carried in front of me in a baby carrier. While he slept and dreamed of kegs of breast milk, I would sweat buckets from his body heat, but at least I could work with the baby strapped to my chest. I was very grateful for laptops, the Internet, kitchen tables and baby carrier.

One scene I recall that rounded up that summer was when I had dashed out the shower to take an urgent call from my publicist and was then suddenly handed a drooling version of my son. Strapped with a towel, open laptop, baby balancing on one arm and a mobile phone in the other hand, I somehow negotiated the crisis. But then the strong whiff of what smelled the opposite of a freshly showered person ruffled my nose. Through the corner of my eye I saw that the trees outside had already begun to change colour towards an autumn haze. This summer was over and the realisation that a quick diaper change was needed brought me back to the room.

Lessons learned

- Becoming a parent is no easy task but you learn a new skill set every day!
- I can't win rock, paper, scissors contests twice in a row!
- Baby carriers are awesome!
- You cannot simply integrate yourself into Bavaria culture by wearing leather pants and drinking beer.

The guide: Every baby is different

The first thing about becoming a father is understanding that your child is an individual and is unique. There can't be a common rule book that applies to each child because they are made of different DNA that creates a never seen before being. Some may sleep easily with background noises while others break out into a raging fit when a pin hits the floor. So the key is to observe and learn their needs and wants as quickly as you can.

If you can manage that then the next step is to anticipate baby's needs to keep him or her happy. Also seek good and correct medical advice before you attempt anything unknown and that you are unsure of.

Chapter 10
The battle of the diaper and one of the greatest business models of all time

Three months of raising a child had its challenges. But each obstacle was met and made us even more prepared for the next. It was the feeling of being Superman, coupled with the systematised skills of Batman and the mind techniques of a Jedi that moulded my abilities as a father.

Super powers aside, I was surrendering to the fact that no matter how fast or how many diapers I changed in a day, there would always be more waiting for me tomorrow.

I remember the first diaper fight. The baby had taken on the persona of Junior Thor and had discovered that he could roll around and make diaper changing more exciting. Kicking and fighting me off seemed to be his area of study. This particular diaper was just about bursting and I took a triumphant moment to wipe the sweat from my brow after securing the fresh diaper in place. I was ready to collapse. However, the problems didn't end as I hadn't realised that I had wiped my sweating brow with poo that had found its way to the back of my hand during the melee. I spent the rest of the day hunting for the source of the smell, in between my other duties, before embarrassingly finding it hours later.

My diaper misfortunes were also augmented with the fact that we were using disposable diapers, so we may have well just been using Euro notes! Disposable diapers are one of the greatest business models on the planet: the more your baby grows, the more it poos, and you get fewer nappies per pack which means more money for the diaper companies. I made serious investigations into developing an affordable, disposable, organic diaper – but like the Holy Grail it is difficult to find!

Time rolled on and autumn swept the country. My German lessons had also come to an end. I said a sad *"auf wiedersehen"* to my foreign friends as I had signed up for the slightly more advanced class that would start a few months later. In the meantime, I watched movies that I knew by heart in English dubbed in German. Although somehow hearing Christian Bale saying "Ich bin Batman!" in his superhero voice didn't quite work for me!

I continued to work from home but knew that soon I would have to travel for business. With a sinking feeling I realised that I would miss my family and some of my son's growing milestones.

Lessons learned

- Diaper manufacturers have created a monopoly on the baby poo market!
- I have multiple nicknames for my son.
- I can say I am Batman in more than one language.

The guide: To diaper management

When engaging in changing a diaper, always remember that this is no game, this is like handling sophisticated machinery with complexities that could make an army of soldiers pass out from the smell. Be prepared, be quick but clinical but most importantly wash your hands after you finish the deed. Also make sure at all costs you do whatever it takes to stop a diaper rash from occurring! Further watch out for babies peeing during a diaper change!

Chapter 11
A bicycle shop, laundry and an endless amount of snow

I had labelled my son a champion as he hadn't thrown up yet. I was busy raving about this to my wife while bouncing away on one of those giant Pilates balls with 'The Champ' himself looking over my shoulder. What I undoubtedly did was catalyse a new beginning of 'Olympic Up Chuck' – the rapidly cooling dribble of puke that cloaked my back that day still gives me chills.

I had jinxed the winning streaked and was made to suffer for my boasting. Once baby gets into vomiting one tends to find odd stains here, there and everywhere. Laundry rounds invariably increase against the onslaught of violent smells that outrank even the fullest diaper but nevertheless managed to linger in my nose and memory for ages.

Six months had passed and we had a progressive child, trying to challenge himself with abilities not made for most his age. This was all good, but it meant he engaged in life threatening events from the falls, bumps and accidents that seemingly never ended.

The final straw for me was while he was trying to master the art of standing. He stood and beamed at his achievement before tipping forward and hitting his head against a very hard table; the achievement was quickly erased in a flood of tears. I couldn't handle the accidents anymore so I headed to the local bicycle store and demanded a baby bicycle helmet, which I found just like the organic cheap diaper simply doesn't exist. The shop owner, a Bavarian who also had a young son, took me aside and gave me the straightforward advice that children grow up and they fall. "This is how they learn," he said. Still wet behind the ears, I responded with the thought that learning would be less painful with a helmet, earning me a pearl of wisdom from the veteran: children need to have the 'feel' for learning. This is the sad realisation of watching your child learn to walk: you can't have learning without pain, and if you shelter them too much from bumps and bruises, you also shelter them from learning.

Winter beckoned and autumn faded away as the first signs of snow signalled a severe winter to come – worse than any I had ever experienced in South Africa. As I stood in the drive way shovelling snow, wearing shorts and a quick dry sports top that drew looks of amusement from passers-by, I began to hate both gravity and snow. This was a new addition to my list of never ending battles.

As I shovelled, kind of like in the diaper experience, I would turn around to see even more snow taking the place of the path I had just cleared. As sweat dripped off my face and my body heat rose with every shovel (which justified me wearing shorts) I simultaneously felt tiny icicles forming on the tip of my nose. My idea of wearing shorts wasn't taken too warmly by my wife who told me to get rid of my South African pride before I lost an appendage to frost bite.

Lessons learned

- Babies have accidents but you can reduce it by watching them like a hawk
- Great business idea number 2: baby helmets
- Shovelling snow can become a never ending job

The guide: Babies learning how to do stuff

Most of the time your baby will be healthy and in a good state during which learning how to touch, hold, roll, stand up, crawl, walk and run will all be part of their development. Your goal is to make sure have a safe environment in which to do this. It's a crazy case of monitoring your baby at all costs as they will take on roles as mini Indiana Jones or Lara Croft. I just realised after mentioning the latter that Sean Connery played Harrison Ford's father in Spielberg's classic adventure series. James Bond as your dad, now that is awesome!

Enjoy the moments as it's a great time to engage with your child. Give them space to learn on their own, but be there to encourage, support and congratulate them too. It is also a period when you will develop a great deal of patience for your child.

Chapter 12
Prams, a blender, hospitals and being knocked out without a punch

With the winter snows firmly on the ground a trip towards the southern hemisphere was definitely on the cards. I had done a few short trips so far, but a long business trip for over a month would be another story. If I could learn how to "pretend to" ski, engage with the odd local Bavarian and workout how to use a pram in the snow, then life wasn't as hectic as it seemed at first glance. For me everything was a challenge, but not so for my wife. She was efficient as you could only imagine a German to be and between us got everything to work. She never had a diaper incident as bizarre as mine and she could operate our pram with the grace of an ice skater in the middle of a snow storm!

I however was a calamitous disaster and handling the pram had led to multiple arguments – mostly between me and the pram. I am not sure what the neighbours thought, but I am sure they knew I was not a local. Watching me angrily stomp around a pram would have confirmed their thoughts.

The pram itself was slick, sophisticated and chosen by my wife. Naturally she had won the closed debate about selecting the pram while very pregnant, ostensibly because the pram fitted into the station wagon like a glove. To me the pram represented a man-made version of the guineafowl if only for my loathing of it. It would take me 15 minutes to fold it and get it into the car and then another 20 minutes to calibrate the correct settings after taking it out of the car. Thirty-five minutes of me looking like a fool and cursing at the four-wheeled object while it glimmered smugly back at me – like a silly, new age dodo. The shameful fact is that my wife could set up and pack away the pram in mere seconds. As for the car seat, I would be fighting with trying to get junior strapped into Batman's version of a baby seat, while it took my wife only 30 seconds to operate the Bat mobile baby seat! Needless to say both baby seat and pram were probably responsible for additions to the grey hairs I suddenly developed.

To make matters worse, I wasn't only bedevilled by car seats and prams. There was a blender that was as sophisticated as a space shuttle that I dared not venture near. Rightly so because it was responsible for making a great mashed up puree that the baby lived on once he moved onto solids. And that my friends, was the beginning of really smelly diapers; be warned! I tried watching the revamped version of the Karate Kid, but I didn't find much to guide me on handling a baby carriage, Batman's baby seat or a blender that was smarter than I was. I did however learn to use the washing machine, which was about five years older than I was. Basically, I got demoted from pram station to laundry duty.

At times I felt like the Inspector Clouseau of fathers – a fumbling idiot of sorts. The baby already had me racing to the emergency ward a number of times from a fall off a chair to biting a berry that may have been poisonous; the list is long and I learned all the shortcuts to the hospital. It was funny and every trip I made felt as though I had aged by the equivalent of a few winters. I did however find other fathers who had similar issues, though not as rife as mine. I heard from a friend who got hit on the head with a cricket bat by his baby and another whose son made contact with cat vomit, which in turn caused him to vomit while cleaning up his baby. I commiserated with them and just nodded in acknowledgement with the understanding that my fate would similarly unfold just around the corner.

Around the corner was a quick knockout punch from Mike Tyson. My son had picked up a stomach virus that gave him the runs and constant vomiting; we did not sleep for three full days! By day four we weren't much better than zombies, but he seemed to be recovering. We were already looking forward to a good night's sleep when the left hook connected. First my wife fell ill and tried to sleep it off. When she called to me from the bedroom, I basically walked into chaos. The baby had oozed out what looked like something from a horror movie (*The Exorcist* comes to mind) and my wife had gracefully joined suit. I managed to keep my cool and called my mother-in-law who rushed over immediately. I reassured her that I was fine, and I asked if she could take the baby to allow us some time to recuperate. It was then that I walked to the bathroom and casually threw up in the sink (from the proverbial right hook); the uppercut arrived as I fainted for the first time in my life, falling and smacking my head against the nearby cupboard. My son was a champ after all!

For a moment I was a kid again, running through fields in a South African veld with guineafowls running all around me. Then slowly the daft things flew away and the veld became a bright white ceiling. I sluggishly retraced what led me to this prone position: wife, baby, family and Germany, in that order. At that moment I connected the dots like a Ridley Scott plot and realised that the baby had transmitted a viral stomach bug that left my poor wife flattened in bed and knocked me out cold.

I recovered in time to embark on the longest business trip away from my family. I was headed to the southern hemisphere where it was warmer and there was much less risk to my health.

Lessons learned

- Baby equipment is expensive and can be highly frustrating to operate.
- Peter Sellers was the best Inspector Clouseau ever!
- One baby can take out two adults faster than most boxers.

The guide: Baby equipment

Baby equipment is something that needs to be carefully chosen and researched. There are pros and cons to everything, including pricing. Furthermore, safety ratings that explain the effects and the quality of products by independent rating setups are very helpful in choosing which or what type of equipment is best for you and the baby. If you are able to do a mix of using online research and physically going to a baby store to test out equipment that would be optimal. The equation of budgeting, researching and choosing quality products will more than often lead to a solution. Again every baby and family have different needs and requirements therefore what equipment you require is specific to you and your child.

Chapter 13
Longest journey in the shortest time and minding your language

Not seeing my family for weeks was not the easiest experience for me, especially now that junior was on the scene. Even though we lived in the tech age, no Internet, mobile or other technology in the world could come close to the real thing.

I did however find that my work turn over improved significantly. Once you get some serious (family) responsibilities under your belt, you tend to cut to the chase in business and get work done just as well, if not better, in a shorter space of time. So I applied this strategy to my everyday work activities while I was travelling, which made the trip successful

On my return what I didn't expect was to see how much my boy had grown in the short space of time that we were apart. I had witnessed his mini growth spurts after taking shorter business trips, but this was the biggest one yet. He matured into a physically bigger individual, was definitely a lot more knowledgeable and, best of all, he never forgot who I was! It was like dealing with a new baby but it was totally awesome though at times I missed the new born persona he had outgrown of.

One of his new developments was a move to start using the potty. A peace treaty of sorts to my never ending battle with diapers. The term for this process is called Potty Training which I think is incorrect; it should rather be called "This is the reason why diapers were invented and why are you parents doing this to yourselves". The training consisted of rapid running between the point of him doing a "Number 2" and the toilet. As charming as the term "Number 2" sounds what often happened between the two points was far from a pretty or nasally-appealing episode. Therefore I would rather spare the specifics and just say that getting your child to the toilet on time is key to this learning procedure. Though we were a long way from moving away from the whole diaper battle it was at least a step forward to ending the conflict!

During one particularly loud and eventful potty training session, the sister-in-law's boyfriend (who was visiting again) popped his head into the entrance of the bathroom after being roused from an ad hoc slumber. His brash inquiry into what going on was met with my evilest of looks. This scared him away as he quickly comprehended the magnitude of the dirty task I was facing in the bathroom.

As the seasons rolled towards summer with a crisp spring thaw, young Thor was fully into walking and talking. The latter was non-stop. There were times when he tired from walking and he would often perch on my shoulders, until he somehow managed to mistake my shoulders for the potty! I never quite got the hang of timing with the whole diaper and potty training issue. For him it was okay wherever he made his business, just as long as he did it and was able to be cleaned up afterwards, if needed. As time passed I soon was able to swiftly clean up a number 2, setup a baby bath in a flash and get him ready for his day with little fuss. Feeding was simple, being a mixture between breast milk and solids. Since I didn't have boobs I was saved half the work there.

Boobs, or mammary glands, despite what most men think were not made for us. Babies own them and will not hesitate to fight for them. As Superman respected Kryptonite, I learned to respect my child's boundaries in the same way.

I became a multi-tasker of note and not by choice. I learned to get up early and start work before sunrise, assist with the morning baby preparations, then get back to my desk for the normal work day. The family support we had helped us survive through it all – they were there when we needed them most and understood our situation. One also can't over-value solid infrastructure – it is priceless and in terms of Germany, it is stereotypically super-efficient. When I look back now, life simply shifted and shaped itself into place for us and we managed to do it all without any major catastrophes.

I always butted heads with challenges compared to my wife's ability to see a solution before the challenge arose. She had the polar opposite set of skills and filled in the gaps that I was lacking. For instance, my attempts to feed the baby with solids often ended with me taking on the role of Pablo Picasso: painting my sons face with food. My wife's solution was to let him feed himself. It worked and from thereon we simply supervised his self- feeding. Then there was the on-going issue of driving with him in the car. I thought the Bat mobile car seat was the issue, but my wife found out that he really wanted to listen to his reggae music. This meant whenever we drove in the car with him we had to have the exact reggae mix playing that we had when we were pregnant with him. On repeat. That CD incidentally now rivals my dislike of the guineafowl, with snow and gravity coming in close behind!

With the baby growing up with two languages, he learned to speak a lot earlier than we had expected. His comprehension and repeating of words was super-fast. So fast that before we could think about what we had said, it was repeated back like a tape recorder – in a baby auto-tuned version.

Cursing or swearing was definitely something to be kept on the down low. I was told by a friend of mine that her child called an aeroplane a duck but somehow dropped the 'd' and replaced with an 'f'. This led to an embarrassing flight as the child kept shouting loudly that they were in a bird that was incorrectly spelt with the f-word. I told myself that I would cut down on my cursing the day my son arrived. It was a bad habit of mine that cultivated in high school, accelerated at university and cemented during my working life. Once, while rushing around with a baby in one arm and my mobile on speakerphone, my world was spinning too fast for my liking – I accidently referred to the excrement of a bull. My son later, out of the blue, called me bull's excrement, a charming way to learn not to say bad words in front of your child.

My father-in-law had told me to take it all in during the first year, because it was going to flash by within seconds. He was right, the little one's first birthday had arrived and it was my introduction to the world of children's birthday parties. As long as there were no purple dinosaurs or clowns resembling *IT* from Steven King's horror classic, such celebrations were not so bad. At the end of even the most challenging day, I can still look forward to a lifetime ahead full of memories and adventures.

It has been a mad adventure of nine months and junior's first year, but it is a time that I will never forget. And to prove that the experience wasn't all that bad, it didn't take long before baby number two was on the way. But that's a story for next time.

Lessons learned

- Every child is different. They have their own needs, wants and preferences.
- Catering to certain preferences may mean a life of driving with reggae music.
- Potty training is a messy and smelly process.
- Being called bulls' excrement by your child is a clear lesson not to use bad language in general.
- It feels like losing the word "the" from your vocabulary when trying not to curse or use profanity!
- The first year of having a baby goes by fast. Remember to lift your head out of survival mode often to enjoy the view.
- I have learned more about life in one year than I did in my first 29 years. And my teacher was nearly the same height as Yoda!

The guide: Potty training and building a vocabulary

The key to potty training is to be observant and try to understand what your child is facing. Toilet use is something that adults (hopefully) take for granted, but represents a whole new skill set for your young one. When junior starts to take an interest in your toilet activities, encourage their curiosity and relate it using words that they already know. That said there are some parents who just throw their kids into the deep end without waiting for the child to give them a sign. Different strategies will work for differed children, so be open minded. There is no specific timing for potty training to begin. Some parents avoid for as long as they can and some encourage it. Make sure you get proper advice from your child's paediatrician when dealing with this process. Also be aware that this process is a 24 hour one including needing preparation for when the baby is asleep at night. Potty training is a messy procedure but it is the first step towards a diaper free environment!

Cursing or the willy-nilly use of foul language in front of your child is never good. They pick it up and repeat everything whenever and wherever it is most embarrassing. So save the blushes and watch what you say; it is pretty simple with a bit of self-discipline. At least then baby will be repeating more appropriate words in their initial steps towards proper dialogue. Read a lot (to them), communicate in bundles and have fun building up a library of words with your child.

Part 3: Tales and adventures of other dads

Any challenges or events that happened when your new born first arrived?

He had a hectic birth so he needs to be close to mum mostly. It is quite difficult just understanding what he wants when he cries. Whoever invents a machine that can interpret baby's thoughts or their cries will become an instant billionaire! I would like to also have more time to spend with him as I don't want to miss his first experiences... – **First time father Robert Quarshie, Münster, Germany.**

The initial weeks involve an inevitable steep learning curve and lack of sleep (assuming you've decided that you're going to invest in being an involved father), however there is an interesting emotional journey as you re-evaluate your who you are, what you do and what sort of example you are setting for your family. The reality of providing for a family helps to focus the mind! – **Father of two Owen Burton, London.**

When I was prepping to become a dad, I was surrounded by unsolicited advice from all sides -- mostly from my single friends without kids for some reason. The thing that stood out for me was looking forward to an immediate falling-in-love with the baby when I first got to see him. The disappointment was that this didn't happen for me, and upon reflection I am sure that I am not the only one. Rather, my love for my kid came out of his total reliance on me (and his mum) to keep him comfy and alive! Your kid becomes a treasure that no pre-baby scare stories can over shadow. Rather than resenting the radical changes to my life style as I stepped up to the parenting plate, he is the centre of my world, and I wouldn't have it any other way. – B**orn father Simon Nye, Cape Town.**

What has been some of the funniest moments that you have experienced as a father?

As an expectant father, all I can say is hormones, baby movements and ultrasound pictures...

Hormones: You are going to experience a rollercoaster of emotions from your wife, when it seems they are coming out of left field - it's going to be hard to understand during these times how it's your fault. But hey just put it down to hormones and roll with the punches, it's all worth it!

Baby movements: Feeling and experiencing the movement of your baby while in your wife's belly is a trip, knowing someday that little person will soon communicate with you face to face and grow up to experience life with you.

Pictures: The ability to see your new baby wriggling, twisting, sucking their thumb, kicking, and practicing breathing all before arriving in this world. This will bring intrigue, happiness and a countdown to the day the little guy arrives in your life to touch, hold and love." (At the time of interview) – **Expectant father Troy Evans, San Francisco.**

This really is a tough question, because there are countless moments and they would definitely fill more than one book. But being asked about it, one story comes directly to my mind. My daughter was playing "palace" and ordered everyone around. She told her mother and me what to do and which prince and princess we were supposed to be. And wondering about her own role I asked her: "What about you, who are you going to be?" ...her direct response that left us speechless was - without any hesitation – a simple: "I am the boss!" (*Ich bin die Chefin!*) – **Father of two Oliver Huq, Düsseldorf.**

How do you balance work with being a dad?

"Work life balance is tricky. We try to have a family breakfast every morning which involves Georgina feeding her entire face some food. Then I try making sure I am back for bath time in the evening and I put her to bed. The key is being flexible with the time you have. It also means I am lot more disciplined at work. I used to work from home 1 day a week. But this became tricky the more active she got. It wasn't fair on her or my work when I was half interested in both." – **First time father Marc Mazery, Melbourne.**

I suspect my wife would say quitting my job and starting a new company a couple of months before our first child was born was somewhat challenging. There was an upside - no office to go to so I could be around more. There was however that other thing of having to earn money and get a business off the ground...all fun at the time. – **Experienced father Michael Whitehead, Auckland.**